IT'S ALL **ABOUT** YOU

THE ESSENTIALS OF CREATING, BUILDING, AND MANAGING YOUR ONLINE BRAND

SHAWN BROOKS
DIGITAL BRANDING STRATEGIST

© **2018 Shawn Chandler Brooks**

All rights reserved. No part of this publication may be reproduced, stored in a retrieval system or transmited in any form or by any means, electronic, mechanical, photocopying, recording or otherwise without the prior permision of the publisher or in accordance with the provisions of the Copyright, Designs and Patents Act 1988 or under the terms of any licence permitting limited copying issued by the Copyright Licensing Angency.

Published by:
Shawn Brooks LLC
2121 N Bayshore Dr #903
Miami, FL 33137, USA

Typesetting: Shawn Brooks

Cover Design: Shawn Brooks

A CIP record for this book is available from the Library of Congress Cataloging-in-Publication Data

ISBN-10: 0-578-43545-4
ISBN-13: 978-0-578-43545-9

Printed in USA

What People Are Saying

Shawn Brooks is such an inspirational business leader. He is a branding and marketing genius! Shawn has helped me develop my online brand over the years and his book will help you! I love having the book as a resource to keep me on the right track! Get your copy today!
>   --- **Buffie and Dr. David Purselle, Serial Entrepreneurs**

I'm so excited! I can't wait to share this book with my charity group. Our next step "Marketing Your Brand" is outlined in easy to follow instructions. The content is relevant and sharp – an outstanding resource. Thank you, Shawn Brooks, for creating our successful website and now for this golden book on branding.
>   --- **Tanya Foskey, Administrative Assistant**

Shawn Brooks is one of the masters at bringing a brand to life. This book contains some of his best kept secrets to creating a winning brand. He doesn't just share the details of how to make a brand stand out, he explains the details behind the secret to the success. I love his stories about how he came to be an expert and his vulnerability in sharing his journey. Must read!
>   --- **Silva Harapetian, Media Marketing Specialist**

Shawn Brooks is an absolute genius when it comes to branding and marketing. After reading his book, And following his advice, I saw my clientele grow exponentially. In fact, I'm getting so much new business I've had to hire extra help. Do what this guys says, and you WILL see results.
>   --- **Tamara Ansari, Attorney at Law**

What can I say about this book? To begin all the details of what you need, to setup and manage an online brand. Many make the mistake of not utilizing online platforms and help guide, well Shawn has done some really intensive research in his new book that will truly help you "Create, Build and Manage your online Brand". As pioneer in branding Shawn was able able to put the essentials needed to Build that Online Brand. I give this book a five and half star, the half star is for his selection of the perfect name for the book. "Told you, every detail he thinks about includes branding."

--- Vitos St. Rose, Creative Director

This is an instructional manual to success, written in plain terms, it teaches us not only Branding but how to start a business. I have been hesitant to join social media platforms, for variety of reasons. This book has shown me the need to create a social media presence for me to develop my personal brand. An easy read. Get this book!

--- Curtis V. Hodge, Director of Lighting

In this time of economic uncertainty, Shawn provides a proven avenues for success. Shawn's thought provoking experiences attest to his resiliency and passion for success and the same passion comes forth in this literary masterpiece as he share his strategies with all.

--- L.R. Burnett-Hill, Business Woman, Author

This is the best "education" and advice that I have received on this topic -- all in one place. A lot of great information and practical advice. It made me personally stop and think, take stock -- and then gave me practicable ACTION STEPS. I am really glad that I purchased it; and, I am already making better decisions and choices that are showing results. I am also going to recommend it to others.

--- Dr. Beverly Scott, CEO, iyai.org

Dedication

To My Creator God Almighty who gifted my life.

To my parents Diane Foskey and Keith Brooks who gave me birth.

To Lucille (Grandmother) and Annie Ruth (Godmother) who gave me guidance.

To Friends Lamont Snead, Vitos St.Rose, Josie Terry, Silva Harapetian, and Curtis Hodge who gave me friendship.

To My kids Ramone, Steven, Tyler, Sydney, and Shawn who gave me desire.

To My Wife Shawnda who gave me effortless support.

To All that know me who gave me motivation.

Contents

Preface	11
Acknowledgements	13
About the Author	17
Introduction	18
Why You Need a Brand Image To Succeed Online	20
What is a Brand?	22
Why Do You Want To Start an Online Brand	28
Creating an Online Brand	32
How to Come Up with a Mission Statement	41
Establish Your Company Name	45
Creating Your Logo	49
Where to Use Your Logo	55
Building Trust	60
Marketing Your Brand	67
How to Manage Your Brand Reputation	90
Conclusion and Recap	93
Final Words	97

Preface

Learn the Essentials of Creating, Building, and Managing your Online Brand. Find Out The Exact Steps To Gaining Trust And Authority In The Market Using The Power of Branding!

Your brand is really important because your brand is your identity. It's what you stand for. Without a clear sense of identity and a clear mission statement, why would people consider following you or working with you? Building the proper brand can increase your exposure, make you memorable, create loyalty, and allow you to set a premium price.

Acknowledgements

I lost my mother at the age of 4. Without a father in the picture my siblings and I were sent to live with my grandmother in an overcrowded house in Aliquippa, Pennsylvania. She was partially blind, a physical condition caused by a fire I once set to the house. I had a difficult childhood.

At almost 50, I realize that the challenges, the suffering, and the disappointments I experienced and the chaos I caused as a child have made me who I am today and I am thankful. But, there were times when I was growing up that I wanted what my friends had; parents, a stable home, toys, brand-name clothes, a way to fit in, and an easy and careless childhood. Instead, I was bullied, teased and was on a path with no direction.

When I was 10, I had one pair of shoes. One day, walking home from school, I took a short cut through the alley and noticed a pair of Nike tennis shoes hanging from someone's trash can. These weren't just another pair of Nikes. They were the popular black canvas Nikes with white bottoms and red fat laces. These were the "in style" shoes. I pulled them out of the trash, noticed the right pair had a hole in the bottom and they were a ½ size too big. I took them anyway.

It felt like I had struck gold that day. I was so excited. The Nike pair of shoes was going to fix my image and make me popular. The days of being bullied for my clothes and teased for my no-brand-name shoes were over. I stayed up all night cleaning the pair and fixing the bottom by placing a piece of wood paneling inside the shoe to cover the hole.

The next morning, I went to school full of swag. The kids noticed. They were all whispering in the hallways and in my classes about my new Nikes until 5th period when my world came crashing down. One of the kids in class yelled out, "Hey, your sock is hanging out from the bottom of your shoe." I looked down and there it was; my stinky, white-turned-dark-gray sock poking out of my shoe. We were poor. We didn't have a washing machine and only one pair of socks to make it through the week. So, we would wear the socks every day and as the sock got dirty we would fold the dirty portion of the sock into our shoes. It prolonged the use of the sock. But, because the Nikes were a ½ size too big and there was a hole the bottom of the shoe, the movement of my foot made the sock slip around my MacGyvered shoe. It was the worst day of my life – worse than anything I had experienced. I punched and broke the glasses of the boy who ruined the only opportunity I had for a popular image.

Because of the way the kids saw me, I was never taken seriously. My clothes weren't hip and my shoes weren't brand names. I was the poor, stinky kid and that's how they branded me. I simply didn't fit in and that affected my image, the way they saw me, the way they treated me and that impacted the way I saw myself. I was overwhelmed, embarrassed and frustrated. Even though I was courteous, smart and giving, still I was a nobody. That was my first experience with image, perception and branding.

It's been almost 50 years and life has changed dramatically since then. I went into the military and grew into a confident man, father, husband and business owner. But, I never forgot that experience and the power of perception. In fact, I credit the success of my business to that experience.

I am on a path to show people how to use branding to change their image through managing other people's perception. This book is my way of sharing with you everything I have learned in my life and career about branding, how to use it and how to make it work for you.

"It's All About You: The Essentials of Creating, Building and Managing Your Online Brand" was inspired by my desire to help people understand the importance of communicating and managing the perception of who they are in business. Your image is you. It represents your core belief system and relates to your goals. Prior to going into business you should know where you want to go and what you want your business to look like. Your image plays a more vital role than you might think.

If you've heard it once, you've probably heard it a hundred times – in life, image is reality. In this new technology driven era, this is truer than ever. Facts don't always matter so much. It's more about the image.

I'm very appreciative to the people who have helped me gain confidence to refine myself and create a whole new image. I have become confident in who I am today and have built a business creating and managing other peoples brand.

I wouldn't have been able to be where I am today without some influential people in my life. My teacher Ms. Moody provided counseling, speech therapy, and constant motivation throughout my schooling. My junior high basketball coach Mr. John Lindsey allowed me to be part of something even though I didn't have the talent to play basketball. My 9th Grade Graphic Arts Teacher Mr. Dennis Drevna introduced me to the world of design. My uncle James Tigner inspired me to want to be a good father. I'm thankful for every person who has ever spoken a word into me. For every word that was spoken, it was taken and applied. I will forever be indebted to you.

About the Author

Shawn Brooks is a brand strategist and entrepreneur living in Miami, Florida who loves sharing knowledge and helping others on the topic of building their brand.

Shawn has worked with over 3,000 customers globally, designed over 500 websites, created over 500(+) logos, designed over 10k pieces of marketing material throughout his career, and has been part of the success of several million dollar brands.

Shawn's proficiency, professionalism and integrity have gained him the trust of high profile celebrities and friendships with public officials and corporate businesses that include Kellogg Co., Marriott International Inc., The Seagram Company Ltd., Aids Walk Atlanta, The NAACP, and Hair Are Us, LLC. Shawn has also worked with Dr. Beverly Scott, *member of National Infrastructure Advisory Council (NIAC)*, Darrelle Revis, *NFL Cornerback and Super Bowl Champion*, Buffie Purselle, *Serial Entrepreneur and Former Cast Member of The Profit*, as well as Silva Harapetian- *CBS contributor, producer and on-air talent*.

If you would like to learn more about Shawn, please visit: www.ShawnBrooks.com

Introduction

To succeed online or in business, you need a brand. It's not enough to simply start spamming the web with content. You need to ensure that you have thought about who you want to be. How you are going to gradually raise awareness of your company? How you are going to introduce customers to your products and services? How are you going to cement the loyalty of those who come across your business? In this book, we will look at how you can create a strong brand and grow it and become recognizable by your logo alone. We'll go through why you need a brand if you're running an online business. We'll look at the basics of what a brand is. We'll look at all the tools and techniques you'll need to create a brand that works for you in a highly effective manner.

Why You Need a Brand Image to Succeed Online?

It is somewhat impossible to succeed online without a brand but doing this is going to be a lot harder and you will seriously be limiting your potential for growth and for profit.

Let's assume for a moment that your business model is predominantly online – let's say that you are selling digital products or affiliate products through a brand. Now in this case, your key objective is to grow the amount of traffic visiting your site, and to then establish trust with that audience so that they will be interested in buying what you have to sell.

This will be highly impossible to accomplish if you haven't first built a brand and layered it into your site and your content.

This is how it works:

Someone finds one of your articles through social media or a Google search, enjoys it and then moves on to other things – no one becomes an 'overnight fan

- During another search or through another post they then find themselves coming across another post or two of yours

- They read this, enjoy it and remember that they enjoyed the last thing you wrote about too

- They then come across you a couple more times and are impressed each time

- They now consider you a reliable/entertaining resource

- The next time they're looking for content in your niche, they will search for their question and your URL

- Perhaps they'll take some time to look around the other content on your site

- They may even then bookmark your site or subscribe to your RSS feed (a type of web feed which allows users to access updates to online content in a standardized, computer-readable format.)

- Likewise they may subscribe to you on social media and/or add their e-mail to your list

- They will then consider buying your e-books/recommended products when they see you recommend them

- If they enjoy the product, they will be much more likely to buy from you again in future.

After this lengthy process, you've now turned a first time visitor into a paying customer.

But note how much more difficult this would be without strong and consistent branding. Without a catchy site name and logo, how would they know that they were reading your website again the second time they found it?

Likewise, without a clear sense of identity and a clear mission statement, why would they consider subscribing?

And if your social media channel is just your personal name with no branding, are they really going to want to follow you?

The same goes for other business models too. Let's say you're manufacturing a product. Having a brand will allow you to market the product and generate buzz for it more effectively but more importantly it will enable you to build on your success. Once you've built a strong brand and people have enjoyed products from you, they will then know to seek out more products from you in the future because they'll expect that they'll be similarly high quality.

Why were people so excited about the Apple Watch recently? It wasn't because it was a smartwatch – there are already hundreds of those on the market.

No, people were excited about the Apple Watch because it was another Apple product and Apple has a reputation for making game-changing technology with fantastic quality construction and elegant interfaces. In other words, it was the brand that sold the Apple Watch more so than the product.

Having a strong brand also makes it much easier for you to market your products and services, creating new opportunities to make people think about your business. At the same time, your brand will also help you to inspire more emotion from your users and customers. With a brand, you'll feel that people will get behind what you're doing and become fans of your products and services. Without a brand, you won't be able to get that kind of loyalty or interest surrounding what you do.

What is a brand?

A brand is a way to clearly highlight what makes you different, and more attractive than, your competitors. Branding is your attempt to harness relationships that will help you succeed. You can benefit enormously by creating an accurate image, especially one that represents true value. Therefore, it is important to always be clear about what your image stands for.

Take for example its Friday night and you are preparing to go to a concert with your friends. You start preparing 2-3 days prior to the event. Why? It's called your brand image. You can't go out looking like anything. You have to represent whom you want the public to perceive you as. You don't have much money in your account but the mere fact that you are about to be noticed in public drives you to overspend in order to create an image. What an interesting fact. People will come up with money to buy "whatever" in order to portray an image. It may be funny but it's all a reality. Case in point you are still trying on clothes, looking in the mirror, and constantly asking "does this look good".

If you can come up with the funds to impress someone just for a night then think about your Image as your future. You have to understand that your image is a vital part of growing any business and needs to be cultivated from the very beginning. Your image has to mimic your personality, your vision, and your goals. Image is everything. It can make or break your business. Take your time and invest in your Image. It's important to the overall success of your brand.

According to Wikipedia, a brand is a 'name, term, design or other feature that distinguishes one seller's product from those of others'.

The word 'brand' itself comes from the way that farmers would once burn their symbols into livestock so that they were identifiably theirs. Your brand should make everything you create and do 'identifiably yours' so that you can build a consistent reputation.

A brand is certainly more than just the logo and name. A brand can also be what distinguishes products from one another. Creating and positioning your brand the right way will build value over time.

What Aspects Make a Brand?

We can also get a better idea for what a brand is by looking at the different aspects that combine to create said brand.

In this book we're mainly focusing on how to create a brand online, so we'll look predominantly at some of the aspects that make a brand on the web in particular.

Aspects of a brand include:

- Your logo
- Your color scheme (will likely be dictated by your logo)
- Your website and web design (again, dictated by your logo most likely, as well as your industry/niche)
- Your advertising (which will feature your logo)
- A jingle (potentially, though not necessarily)
- A 'tagline' (optional)

- A mascot (definitely optional)
- Your products (which should have a consistent design language that makes them look similar)
- Your services (which should have a predictability that makes them reliable and consistent)
- Your content (if you are using content marketing)
- Your social media accounts
- Your 'mission statement' (the end goal of your business
- Your values
- Your persuasive style
- Your attitude

What Aspects Define a Brand?

You can destroy everything positive about yourself with just one inconsistency involving your image. Some important factors in creating your brand image is understanding who you are, what is the core you, and how are you perceived. Have you ever bitten into and apple and it was rotten inside? It wasn't a good feeling. The apple disappointed you. That's what you want to prevent with your image. You have to know that your outer image matches your inner core. Make sure you are not like that apple.

Your brand is also something more substantial. It is how your customers perceive you.

> *"If your brand has a highly perceived value, you will enjoy many more advantages over your competition, especially when it comes to pricing."*

I was once the proud owner of a used car business. As I went to various dealer auctions to buy vehicles I noticed that most of the small dealers were there in their jeans and old dirty t-shirts. The established dealers were represented by the branded images they wore on their shirts. I witnessed that when it came to buying and selling cars at the auction the branded dealers were treated as reputable and honest. Of course we know better. Some of them are the most dishonest people on the planet but remember Image is everything. I convinced our team to try the image concept. As my team and I went back to the auctions with matching branded polo shirts, khaki shorts, hats, and business cards, we started to get the established dealer treatment. The efforts were successful and our new image perception created a new atmosphere for us at the auction.

People are prepared to pay substantially higher prices for items with proven image identity. Why? It's called perceived value. Perceived value is the result of very effective image marketing that results in high brand awareness.

Below are some important attributes that you may need to work on, in order to create an effective brand.

1) Likability

Are you cooperative, pleasant, and unselfish? Do people enjoy being around you? If not, you have to work on it because that's an importance element in any business environment.

2) Punctuality

Do you show up on time? Or do you perpetually roll in 10-15 minutes late, looking at everyone else as if they did something wrong. Are you among the first people to get to a meeting/event or are you the one who is always late or wanting to make the grand entrance. In order to establish a successful brand you have to be punctual. You MUST value time.

3) Humility

Are you the person who only thinks about yourself? Or have you learned how to suppress your ego for the sake of the business? No one likes dealing with a self-absorbed, arrogant, pompous, dogmatic individual. Understand that business is about the others. Your attitude reflects the way you do business.

4) Dependability

Are you reliable? Do you do what you say you're going to do– without hesitation? Do other people think you are reliable or are you the "I'll be there in 5 minutes knowing that it'll be 30? You have to be dependable when it comes to brand management. If clients perceive your business as dependable you will get referrals, which is the best form of client appreciation.

5) Accountability

Can others trust you? Can they depend on you? This is perhaps the most important of all. A great indicator for you to assess your accountability is this: do your friends, family, coworkers ask you or give you important information or tasks?

6) Preparedness

Do you prepare for an event, meeting, or occasion prior to getting there? Can you be relied on to do your homework on whatever subject in order to get the job?

As you can see, a brand is actually many things and certainly not just a matter of creating a fancy logo.

It's your mission and your values that result in products that are a certain standard and this is what will make your customers want to deal with your business again.

Throughout the rest of this book, we'll be looking at how you can tackle each of these points to develop your brand and from there we'll then be focusing on building it up and growing your visibility.

> "Your personal brand is what people say about you when you are not in the room – remember that. And more importantly, let's discover why!"
>
> – Chris Ducker

Why do you want to start an online brand?

Having the right mindset is the most important thing no matter what we do. Whether it's setting up an online brand or learning to play the guitar.

To be honest, when someone wants to know how to set up an online brand it can be a lot more difficult for them than mastering some traditional activities (like sports, for example). That's because not everyone knows what an online brand is and what the exact steps that need to be taken are.

Your Online brand is every business venture where the internet is the main vehicle of: attracting customers, marketing, advertising, processing payments, delivering products (usually), and managing other vital business components.

What do you think is the first step in building a successful brand? It is to understand your 'roots'. Why do you want to build an online brand? What's motivating you? Without a fire in your belly, you won't have the required drive to build a successful business.

So these can be some of the common reasons to build an online brand:

- To earn some extra passive income on the side of a main job.
- To be able to afford to renounce a job you dislike.
- To work on a project that you're passionate about.
- To become financially sound.
- Global access, 24 hours a day, 7 days a week
- Improved client service through greater flexibility
- Cost savings
- Faster delivery of products
- Increased professionalism
- Opportunities to manage your brand from anywhere in the world.

Customers may prefer to visit your website to find out about your products and services, instead of visiting you in person. They will also expect to see your website address and your e-mail on business cards and other promotional materials.

Online Brand Opportunities

How you manage your business online will depend on the products or services you offer. You may be able to use the internet to:

- Run an online shop
- Manage your suppliers
- Communicate with your customers, and get their feedback on your business
- Offer services online

- Allow customers to make reservations or appointments online
- Manage your finances, such as online banking, tax and employee pay
- Research competitors.

Are these things stopping you?

Now that we've identified what's driving you, let's figure out what's holding you back. Before we get started, let's debunk some myths and excuses entrepreneurs make.

"Starting an online brand is expensive"

Totally false. Years ago, starting a business was expensive. To connect with customers you needed a physical location, which could easily cost over $1,000 per month.

Today, the risk of building a business is greatly reduced. Anyone can start a business online for under $10, and serve the billion people around the World who have an Internet connection.

"Building an online brand takes a long time"

Wrong. In fact, by the end of this guide you'll have all the fundamentals to build your online brand. Building your customers and traffic does take time, but it's part of the journey. If you don't think you have enough time to build an online business, then you're right – you probably don't. But even the busiest people make time for the things they truly want.

One extra hour per day is 365 extra hours per year, which is the equivalent of 9 weeks of full time work. What can you achieve in 9 weeks?

"But isn't it really hard to make an online brand successful?"

It depends. It mostly depends on how well informed you are, on the niche you choose, and how you approach it. People who are near-clueless about online marketing make $1,000s just months after setting up a Instagram account, a personal blog or YouTube channel. They were the lucky ones.

The difficulty with building an online business comes down to how well informed you are and your 'roots'. With the right knowledge, it's quite easy.

> " It's important to build a personal brand because it's the only thing you're going to have. Your reputation online, and in the new business world is pretty much the game, so you've got to be a good person. You can't hide anything, and more importantly, you've got to be out there at some level. "
>
> – Gary Vaynerchuk

Creating an online brand

Before you start any business, you need to decide what products or services you will provide. Starting a free online business is no different. Start by thinking about your interests, passions, and skills. Do you have a hobby you can turn into a business? Do you have knowledge or skills other may want or need?

It's important to choose an idea that you can stick with as opposed to searching for the cheapest or most profitable option. Building a business you're passionate about increases the chances that it will succeed and that you'll enjoy it.

Many people believe starting a business is a mysterious process. They know they want to start a business, but they don't know the first steps to take. In this chapter, you're going to find out how to get an idea for a business--how you figure out exactly what it is you want to do and then how to take action on it.

As you make your list, don't filter out any ideas initially. You never know what obscure or odd idea could become a successful business. Later you'll do research to identify the most viable and affordable ideas. But at the brainstorming point, write them all down.

The biggest mistake that first-time online entrepreneurs make is choosing a good idea in a bad niche, or a bad idea in a good niche.

Similarly, Far too many ambitious people venture out to build a business out of travel or recipe blogging. Those niches are so saturated that it's virtually impossible to make a significant amount of money from them today.

So, what sort of online business should you create?

A good niche will tick all of these boxes:

- You can take care of it.
- You must be able to become the authority on it.
- You must be able to differentiate yourself.
- You must fulfill a need.
- Your niche must be commercial.

Let's go through each of these in detail, as this is incredibly important to get right.

#1 You must take care of your niche

Would you be willing to write about your niche every day for six months without being paid a penny? If you can answer 'yes', then you can tick this box and move on.

Growing your online business takes time. There will be times where you work your butt off with very little to show for it.

That's why you need to care about your niche. When you care, you will have the willpower to get you through the tough times. Passion can also be smelt from a mile away. If you don't care, your readers or customers won't care either.

#2 You must be able to become the authority in your niche

What can you be the best in the World at?

While it may be unrealistic right now to be the most authoritative blogger on raw food, you probably could become the authority on raw food desserts.

There are many reasons why this is important. They all boil down to the fact that online business is a winner takes majority game. The majority of traffic and revenue in any niche will be going to the market leader. All of their competitors will then be fighting over the minority.

The minority is a tough place to be. In my opinion, you're better off owning the majority of a smaller niche than the minority of a massive niche.

Choose a niche that you are credible and able to be the authority in.

#3 You must be able to differentiate yourself

For instance, a pharmacist with a passion for understanding how different foods and skincare products affect the body at a biological level is willing to start a business in that area.

Now, there are a ton of health food and skincare bloggers and online businesses out there. What makes this pharmacist different?

Few skincare bloggers can look at the list of ingredients on the back of a shampoo and understand how each chemical or ingredient interacts with the body. A trained pharmacist will not only have the credibility and authority, but she also has her differentiator.

#4 You must fulfill a need

Do people in your desired niche have a problem? Can you solve it for them? Does solving it involve a commercial transaction taking place?

If you can't confidently say yes to all three, adjust your niche idea.

#5 Your niche must be commercial

While interest and passion are important, you also need to choose an idea that has a market. If no one is interested in what you have to offer, it doesn't matter how good you are at it, you won't have a business.

Finding a good Niche

Once you've got a niche idea, it's time to evaluate the level of competition that you're up against.

Having competitors is a good thing. They will motivate you to perform better. Having competitors also helps to confirm that your niche is viable – as you can see whether what they're doing is working or not.

Why should you concentrate on a niche audience first, instead of products? Here are two solid reasons:

- Products come and go, but niche audiences stick around forever. If you've ever been promoting a product profitably and then had it decline in popularity (or pulled off the market entirely), you know what I'm talking about.

- When you choose a niche audience and take the time to understand their needs a whole new world of options open up to you. You switch from struggling to find ideas for products, to instantly knowing exactly the types of products you should be promoting – because they're in tune with your niche audience's needs.

So how do you Get Started Finding a Niche?

Follow these 4 straightforward steps:

1. Brainstorm an audience. You can do this in a few ways:

Choose an audience that you represent yourself (for example, male university student between 18 – 25 years old, or middle-aged professional male)

Choose an audience that you gravitate toward (in other words, people you like hanging around with).

Work backwards, and choose an audience by first picking a niche topic that interests you. This could involve picking a niche like "photography", then doing research on sites like Porfessional Photographers of America (PPA) to figure out resources rquired to getting in the photography business.

2. Identify the problems your niche audience has. This involves doing research into the problems, challenges, pain points, aspirations, and desires of your audience. There are many places online that you can find this information, including niche forums, how-to websites, popular blogs, and "trend" websites.

3. Pick out the most profitable problems. Not all problems are created equal. Some problems your audience will gladly pay to solve; others will be a hard sell. You need to understand the difference, and you can do so using "filters" such as:

- The number of monthly searches related to a problem
- The number of searches that imply intent to solve that problem
- The stability of search terms related to that problem
- The amount of good-quality, free information on the Web

4. Understand profitable problems deeply. It's not enough to simply know that, for example, females between 18 and 34 are looking for the best virgin hair. You need to find out what exactly they want in a virgin hair, and the problems they have with current suppliers. There's more to it then simply finding your niche, however. You also need to understand the language they use in describing their ideal solution, so you can echo that language back to them in your ad copy, sales page copy, etc.

Conclusion:

If you're sick of playing "online pinball", you need to take a step back and re-assess your strategy for building an online brand.

The strategy that has worked well for me (and lots of world-class companies) is to choose a niche audience to serve, then dive in and understand that audience's problems deeply. By doing so, a new world of profitable opportunities will open up to you!

Competitor Analysis in the niche

The success of an online business is highly dependent on the niche (or market) you choose to do business. Before you build a web site or a product; you have to find niches which are profitable.

By doing a series of analysis you can quickly filter and decide the profitable nature of a particular niche. Looking into the real statistics and by seeing the audience behavior you can penetrate into a market very well without hassles.

- Find Niches by Keyword Analysis.

Keywords are the major source of traffic. When it comes to search engines like Google, Bing, Yahoo – they are purely driven by keywords.

How the people search? What information people are looking? These data helps you to make the best decisions ever.

There are lots of tools available in the market to perform keyword analysis.

The software is built specially for Niche Analysis. Right from keywords, search statistics – you get all the data in hand with simple clicks. All you have to do is search your keywords and start the analysis. The online tool suggests the best keywords to use.

By doing keyword analysis, you get to know the market behavior and the audience behavior – if you are seeing lot of demand for a particular set of keywords you can definitely get into the market.

- Avoid Crowd by Competition Analysis.

Keyword analysis helps to pick the profitable market where there is demand! It is good to have a set of keywords (instead of having only one) by doing the analysis – once done; you have to identify the competition level for each keyword.

The micro niche finder helps you to see the competition level for each keyword as well as the search trends. It also checks for the availability of domain name for those profitable keywords, if available you can quickly get a domain name for the selected keyword.

- Try to pick keywords which have good number of monthly search volume say 5000+ searches – that shows the market demand.

- If there are domain names left, the competition level is pretty low.

Further, once you have identified the keyword you can do a Google search and look over the top 10 pages. Use the SEO Quake Firefox Add-on or the Keywords Everywhere Chrome Add-on and analyze the top your results – this gives various data related to each domains listed on the SERP (search engine results page).

- The number of in-links, pages indexed in search engines and the domain age are few of the important parameters that you have to check. When you see such low end web sites on the home page (top 10 results) then you can definitely pick that keyword.

You can repeat these 2 steps – Keyword Analysis + Competition Analysis until you find a high demand low competition niche.

- Look For Problems & Profitable Audience.

The final step in this process – identifying the problems in the niche and nature of audience. This analysis helps to understand the target "audience need" and their nature so that you can build your site or product according to their needs.

- List down the user problems in the niche by searching the web.

- Pick hot problems and make a solution through your web site or product.

- Show your web site or product as a solution to the audience.

Further, you can look into the market on existing products or solutions which gives much better ideas. You can also decide the niche based on the success of these existing products and based on the users comments/reviews available on the web.

> " Building a profitable personal brand online is not a sprint, and something that happens over night. Don't aim for perfection early on. Instead allow your brand to evolve naturally over time and focus on providing massive value and over deliver to your target audience. Then you will get more clear over your message and brand as well. Always remember that! "
>
> – Navid Moazzez

How to Come Up With a Mission Statement

Many brand professionals who are trying to teach how to build a brand begin by focusing on creating a logo. That's not what we're going to be beginning with however as actually the logo you end up creating will be utilizing your mission statement and your values (as well as your industry).

As we've touched on briefly already, it is your values and goals that will truly unify all your activities, products and services. These values should be at the core of everything you do as a business because that is what's going to ensure that you stand out from the crowd and that's what's going to create the consistency that your customers and clients can rely on.

Apple's Values Statement and Why They're Successful

To go back to Apple again (why not, they are fantastic at branding after all), it's clear from looking at their products that they have some very specific values and goals. They are trying to bring products to market that make technology personal, accessible, fashionable and cool. At the same time, they clearly believe very strongly in making things that are high quality, that work well every time and that feel like they're made of good materials.

On top of all this, Apple has a track record of inventing the products we 'didn't know we needed'. They don't make a diverse variety of products but the new products they do introduce often create entirely new product category.

It's no exaggeration to say that it is this what has made Apple successful. Because of those values and those goals, every product that Apple has made has created a huge storm and the experience that customers have had with those products has been hugely positive. As a result, the brand has gone from strength to strength. When people see that little white Apple logo, they know that it represents all those things: quality, innovation, reliability, fashion and more. Some Apple fans are actually verging on being obsessive in their appreciation of Apple and will actively seek to get as many of their products as possible simply because they feel that they too share these values.

Finding Your Values

Of course you are not Steve Jobs and your company is not Apple. It's unlikely you're going to gain quite the recognition or quite the clout that Apple has. And you probably don't have the range of products, or the budget of Apple – (but you are you and you are your brand, you're unique, you have your own values and you too have the power to impact the market.)

Still though, simply by having a commitment to doing what you do better than anyone else, you can still make a splash and impress everyone you do business with. If you run a website for instance, then focus on making sure that the content you publish is always funny, or always more in-depth and thoroughly researched than the competition. Set yourself apart by delivering something that people can't get elsewhere.

Likewise, think about your long-term goals. Why did you get into this business in the first place? Which aspects of it make you truly excited? Where do you see yourself in 10 years time?

This is where a lot of people might be scratching their heads and thinking 'I just want to get rich'. That's a legitimate response but you're probably going to have to go a little deeper if you really want to resonate with your audience. Why did you get into this business in the first place as opposed to another? What is it that you do well that makes you think that you can stand out from the crowd and succeed?

If you're still scratching your head and thinking that you chose this business model because it was easier or because it was 'there', or that you're simply going through the motions and not really bringing anything new to the table… then you need to sit down and reassess your whole business model. This is important not only because you want to create a strong brand but also because you want to succeed. Find that 'extra something' you can offer and then come back to this process.

Writing Your Mission Statement – Your Promise

Now you have a good idea of what your goal is and of what sets you apart, you can consider writing down your mission statement in order to formalize that in a bite-sized chunk.

The objective of a mission statement is to answer the simple question: 'what do you do?'. At the same time though, you should think of this as a promise to your customers/clients and as a way to share your values.

When answering the question 'what do you do', remember that the answer is not 'make hats'. Here the trick is to focus on your 'value proposition' which means determining what it is that you do to create value. Instead of 'making socks' then, your mission statement would be something along the lines of: 'Keeping feet warm in a stylish manner that builds confidence'

Much more inspiring!

Mission statements are generally very short with the average being somewhere between 20 and 25 words. The very shortest is probably from TED which is simply: 'Ideas worth spreading'.

Some other examples of mission statements include:

Ritz Carlton: We pledge to provide the finest personal service and facilities for our guests who will always enjoy a warm, relaxed, yet refined ambience.

Google: To organize the world's information and make it universally accessible and useful.

Microsoft: To help people and businesses throughout the world realize their full potential.

Coca-Cola: To refresh the world, to inspire moments of optimism and happiness, to create value and make a difference

Note that your mission statement is not likely to be something that you use outwardly to promote your brand but versions of it will go on your website and may be used to help motivate and inspire your staff. It will certainly help to write something down before moving forward.

Establishing Your Company Name

Before you go any further, you will also need a name for your company or website. If you already have a name that you're happy with, then you can skip past this chapter. Otherwise, this can be a stumbling block for many people so it's worth taking some time to think about.

When choosing a company name you need to make sure that what you come up with is going to be unique and that it's going to be memorable. At the same time it should also describe something about your business *and/or* about your goals and your attitude.

It's also useful – especially if you are creating a blog as your business – to choose a name that is going to be at least somewhat descriptive of what it is you do.

If you think about some of the biggest brands in the world then you might find that this isn't really the case. 'Apple' is hardly the name you would instantly associate with computers, 'Virgin' is certainly not a name that says much about what that company does and 'Nike' is just a completely random jumble of letters.

In these cases, the company name is more about creating a 'feel' that speaks to the attitude of the business. 'Apple' suggests different and 'fresh'. 'Virgin' suggests youthful, playful and not afraid to ruffle feathers. 'Nike' is strong and simple, just like the logo. Look for words that are evocative and descriptive and make sure you pick something that reflects well on your business.

While you can pick a company name that evokes the kind of attitude you want to be known for, it does often help to choose something descriptive simply because you won't have the marketing clout of those big companies. If your website is a tool for people to measure their fitness and you call yourself 'TheFitnessStatTracker' then you won't need to explain what your company is about and it will be easier for people to search for you. Of course you could make this more stylish by shortening it to 'Fit, Stat, Track' or 'FitStatTrack'.

You might also choose to use a description right in your company name: for instance 'Shawn Brooks Design' or 'Shawn Brooks Photography'. This way you still get the abstract appeal of a non-descriptor but you also tell people what your site or business is about.

Another option is to pick one name for your website and another name for your company. That way you might have a website called 'Making Money is Fun', run by a company called 'Money International'. This can help you to branch out in future and has a number of advantages but it also comes with some drawbacks. A good example of a company with multiple brands would be Microsoft which is a brand in itself, as is Windows and Xbox. In Microsoft's case this has been quite useful as the Xbox brand has managed to avoid some of the flack that often gets associated with Microsoft products.

Defining Your Company Name

There are a few more things to bear in mind for your company name.

One is memorability: how easily will people be able to remember your company name or website? This is particularly true if you want to get direct traffic by people typing your URL into their browser. If your name isn't memorable, try something else.

You may wish to use your own name to sell under – which makes a lot of sense for a personal brand. We'll look more at the strengths and weaknesses of going this direction later. Bear in mind though that you can still create a personal brand without that having to be the name of your business or website.

Finally, think about your initials. This is important to:

a) avoid an embarrassing acronym (it's also worth checking what your name means in other languages!)

b) and because letters at the start and end of the alphabet will be easier to find in lists. That latter point shouldn't be a big determining factor when you choose your name but it is something to keep in mind.

Getting a Website

Once you have the name for your brand and/or business, the next thing you need to do is to get web hosting and a domain name which will give people a way to find you.

This might also influence your decision when picking a name for yourself – as if yourname.com is taken, you might want to get creative.

In order to get your website up and running, you need three things:

- **A domain name** – This is the address that people will type into their browser to access your website. For example, www.yourwebsite.com is our domain name.

- **Web hosting** – This is the 'web space' where you upload your website's files to. When someone types in your domain name it serves up web pages from your web host. Think of it like a hard disk drive on the Internet.

- **A content management system (CMS)** – Instead of having to code every page on your website in HTML, a CMS enables you to add pages and make design changes without having to write any code. WordPress is a free CMS, and also happens to be one of the best.

You can get all three of these up and running in a matter of minutes using a web hosting company called GoDaddy.

Choosing a good web hosting company is extremely important. It determines the security, speed, uptime, and overall performance of your website. Fortunately, i've done much of the hard work for you.

Godaddy is my favorite affordable web hosting company. I use them for virtually all of my websites, and I have never had any major downtime or problems.

They offer new customers a free domain name (when you buy a website hosting package first), as well as the ability to install WordPress in one click. In other words, you can have everything you need to set your online business up in under 5 minutes for less than $15 per month.

So, how do you get started? Head over to GoDaddy.com

Creating Your Logo

Now you know who you are, you will be able to start showing that to the world with a stylish logo that encapsulates that and which you can then use in all of your products and across all of your marketing. Note that this does still apply to personal brands – just take a look at any of the big name bloggers and they will still have some form of logo.

What Makes a Good Logo?

A logo is essentially an image – often incorporating your company name – which will act like a 'calling card' so that people can easily identify your creations and so that you can easily remind them of who you are.

Popular examples of logos include the Nike, Mercedes, Best Buy, Apple and McDonalds. There are so many to list but as your searching the internet, walking in the mall, or driving around town pay close attention to the brand logos and colors. This concept is a way to give you an idea of what a logo looks like and how its used.

Your objective will be to create a brand image which people will be able to use to instantly identify you.

The process of coming up with a logo though is a little harder than you might think. The main reason for this is simply that your logo will play such an important role in defining your business going forward and in creating marketing opportunities for you. If you get this wrong, then you could well be 'stuck' with a logo that doesn't represent you well for a long time (rebranding isn't easy). Just as naming your child can seem like an impossible task, so too can creating your logo.

To help you get started, there are a few criteria that a good logo should fulfill. Make sure that your logo meets these and you'll be along the right lines.

A good logo should:

- Be unique and different – this is important to ensure you're identifiable by your logo but it's also important to ensure you're not infringing any trademarks (we'll get to that)

- Avoid clichés (like puzzle pieces, globes and lightbulbs which have been badly overdone and now appear highly derivative)

- Be appropriate for your industry/niche/subject matter

- Be versatile enough to be used in a variety of different places – avoid thin lines which won't show up on some backgrounds

Be simple enough to recreate – if people start doodling your logo in their notebooks you're getting free publicity

Now you have your specifications, you can start the actual planning stage…

Creating The Concept for Your Logo

Before you open up any software, you first need to get an idea of what your logo is going to look like and where you're going with it. We know what we're aiming to achieve with a logo now and we know what makes a good logo. Next we just need some ideas to start building off.

The first place to start often is with a 'mood board'. A mood board is essentially like a collage except you're going to focus on placing lots of different images on it, with the main objective being to create a collection of images relating to your business and your brand that will serve as inspiration.

You can do this either with software or by printing out the images and sticking them down. This way, you can then collect:

- Images of other logos you like the looks of
- Images relevant to your niche/industry
- Images that relate to your mission state/values
- Things you simply like the looks of

Collect as many of these as possible and that way you will find that common themes start to emerge and that you start to get a good feeling for the artistic direction you need to take. You can then start combining elements, color palettes and more to come up with something new.

Playing off your company name is also another option. In most cases you will include the name of your company in the logo and then edit the font or turn specific letters into images.

A great example of this is the logo of Ramone Photography I created for my son who started a photography career. The logo uses the lens of the camera to create the "O" of the brand name.

Example: : Logo sample using camera to create the letter "O"

When creating your logo be very careful and make sure your font is not to thin. Because if you wanted to use your logo as a watermark on a video you were making for instance, you would need to include some black background to make it legible. Simply bulking out the text easily solves that issue.

Some logos will also incorporate a symbol or even a character 'mascot'. You can choose to incorporate something like this as well if you like but make sure that it remains easy to reproduce, versatile and unique.

If you're still struggling to come up with ideas, then take a 'brainstorming' approach and simply draw as many different ideas as you can. Even if you think the idea is stupid, draw it anyway. Eventually you will start to see elements that you like and you can then recombine these to create something imaginative and original.

Finally, don't aim to create one idea. Instead, come up with a few different options for your brand and then try testing it by showing it to people and getting feedback. This is important as often we are too close to our own business and our own creations to view ourselves objectively. Your logo is not for you – it is for your audience. So show the images around and let your customers, your friends or even passers-by in the street and get them to vote on the best one.

Creating Your Logo

You have two options when it comes to creating your logo:
1. Design it yourself (difficult if you don't have any design skills).
2. Outsource (cost money).

Let's talk about each method.

Designing a Logo Yourself

In order to design a logo yourself, you'll need a program like Adobe Illustrator available at http://www.adobe.com/products/illustrator.html.

I can't run through every single step of the process but if you like to learn the basics, you'll find lots of tutorials on YouTube.

What you want to do is to actually make the logo so that it's in a form that will be useable online.

This means turning it into an image file that will look high quality and that will allow you to edit it to use online in various different capacities.

Note that when you create your logo, you need to make it using vector software. When you create a JPG, Bitmap or PNG in Illustrator, this is what's known as a 'raster file' meaning that it consists of lots of individual pixels in a file.

A vector file is different because it essentially works as a 'map' and a set of instructions which define the direction of different lines, the angle and the weight. In other words, it's almost like the 'code' that tells the software how to draw the image.

This has multiple advantages. For starters, it means that you can resize the image to any dimension and not lose any quality. This is important because you might one day find that you need to use your logo on top of a billboard.

Please remember: Vector files are important because they allow you to edit the image without making a mess of things. With a vector image you or your designer or the print company will be able to select any line and then make it wider, change the angle, and change the color.

Outsourcing Your Logo Design

Now let's take a look at outsourcing your logo. This is the best option but obviously requires some investment.

Here is a list of websites where you can get your logo designed:

>**http://shawnbrooksdesign.com** - you can review portfolio and request to get an instant quote.

>**http://99designs.com** - you can start a logo design contest and "crowd source" the design.

>**http://fiverr.com** - a great place to get logos created for just $5. Be prepared for long waits though, designers typically have a large que of orders because the pricing is cheap.

>**http://upwork.com** - an all-rounder outsourcing/freelance website to post jobs.

When outsourcing to designers, make sure you are clear and specific on your instructions and request your logo in the following formats (.ai,.eps, .png, and .jpg). Designers will usually ask a number of questions to understand your business so that they can create a logo that reflects it. The additional files will save you time and money when it comes to design and printing of your marketing collateral.

Protecting Your Trademark

For a brand to be effective, it's very important that no one else be trading using the same name. This is why you need to ensure you protect your brand by getting it patented once you've chosen a company name and a logo.

You can do this by visiting the US Patent and Trademark Office at **www.uspto.gov.** Here, you'll be able to check that your trademark isn't already patented and then patent it yourself for a fee (not more than a few hundred dollars). This will last for ten years, at the end of which you will need to renew your trademark.

When you create a website or write an article, this is going to be instantly protected by copyright and that copyright protection will last until after your death. This is not the same with a trademark – which needs to be actively sought out and renewed. If you're going to be investing a lot into promoting your brand though, then this is definitely an investment worth making.

Personal branding is about managing your name — even if you don't own a business — in a world of misinformation, disinformation, and semi-permanent Google records. Going on a date? Chances are that your "blind" date has Googled your name. Going to a job interview? Ditto.

– Tim Ferriss

Where to Use Your Logo

Hopefully after doing all this you will have a logo that you're happy with. The next question though is: how do you use it?

More Materials to Create

A logo is essentially an image – often incorporating your company name – which will act like a 'calling card' so that people can easily identify your creations and so that you can easily remind them of who you are.

To start with, you might want to try creating some materials that you can use alongside your logo and that will likely come out of the logo too.

For instance, if you are going to be using any type of video marketing or if you will be vlogging on YouTube, then you may want to create a video opener. This is a short animation, often with music, that will play right at the start of your videos to once again tie them altogether. Often the animation will feature the logo in some way or another and very often it will simply be an animation of the logo either moving around or being constructing in some form.

Likewise, you may want to look into creating a business letterhead which you can use when communicating with clients and/or some business cards with your logo on. Already you're seeing how useful and versatile a good logo can be – and this way, every interaction you have with someone will become a chance to reinforce your brand and to help build recognition.

Your Logo Defines your Website

One particularly big aspect of your branding that you will also need to create is your website. Your website will serve as a portal and shop window for your business, as well as an advert and representative of your business and much more. If your website doesn't inspire confidence and isn't memorable then you will miss out on countless marketing opportunities and huge growth potential.

What's interesting is, if you are an Internet marketer or blogger, your website is pretty much your entire business model. If you're making money from advertising on your website or through sales of digital/affiliate products, then it's crucial that your website leave a lasting impression so that customers come back to it.

In this case, simply having your logo at the top of your site is not enough. Logos and banners will typically go at the top of a website because…

a) that fits in with the 'F Zone' (which is the region we are most likely to look when we visit a new site)

b) experience teaches us that we should look at the top for titles and branding

But the fact of the matter is that most people just aren't that interested in logos and banners. Most of the time we visit a website because we're interested in the content of a specific article. So, as soon as we land on the site, we will scroll down to the text and we will skip past everything else. If you want people to recognize your site next time they visit then you need to differentiate your site in more ways than through the logo alone.

How do you do this then?

One answer is to use the same color scheme and design sensibilities you do in your logo *throughout* your entire site.

Take Virgin for instance. Virgin is a huge brand, recognizable by its red and white logo. Virgin's brand is actually *particularly* important too because it is the unifying feature throughout multiple different branches of business.

Now if you take a look at two of their websites (the main 'Virgin' website and the 'Virgin Active' website) you will notice that they have something in common – liberal use of the 'Virgin red'.

As well as quite a lot of white text. This way, no matter which part of the page you are on, you will be reminded that this is a virgin website and the brand will be constantly reinforced.

The same goes for your own site then: try to include call backs to your logo through your choice of color palette, through your background and even through the typeface you use. At the same time, just ensure that your website is recognizable and interesting (without being distracting) no matter which page you're on or how far you've scrolled down. If your site could very easily be any other site in your niche, then you need to think about strengthening its brand identity.

Creating a Personal Brand

Looking at the Virgin website you might also have noticed something else that is very distinctively 'Virgin' – an image of their CEO Richard Branson.

As well as his Virgin Brand, Richard Branson has also been somewhat successful in creating a 'personal brand'. By putting his face and personality at the forefront of much of his marketing and even some of his products, Richard has created an association between himself and his business.

This is something that lends itself particularly well to online business. If you run a website or blog, then you might well use your name as a byline after writing blog posts or you might even appear in videos. Some people will even use their own name as their website name and might use themselves to promote their products. Take a look at Pat Flynn for instance – the owner of Smart Passive Income – whose banner reads 'The Smart Passive Income Blog with Pat Flynn'. Likewise, Buffie Purselle (who owns Just Being Buffie and Buffie The Tax Heiress) has effectively built her business around her own name.

If you are selling a fitness product or writing a fitness blog and you happen to be in great shape, then you can use this to your advantage in order to promote your product and to show that it works.

Attaching yourself to your brand or creating an entirely personal brand is often a good strategy as it helps to build trust (more on that later) and puts a face to the name. At the same time, people are 'programmed' to be very good at recognizing faces and names and as such you can instantly make yourself more memorable by letting people meet the personality behind the website/company.

Some people won't feel comfortable putting themselves forward in such a way and exposing themselves. They may prefer to shy away from the spotlight. Either strategy is fine, just remember that creating a personal brand is a viable option if you want to make your company even more memorable.

Being Everywhere

The next thing to do with your brand online is to make sure that you are everywhere. This essentially means that you should be on every social media platform, that you should have links all around the web and that generally you should ensure that your potential customers are encountering your brand at every opportunity.

To help your customers find you, you want to create as many in-roads as possible and that means that you should have a Twitter account, Facebook page, Google+ page, YouTube channel, Instagram account, Snapchat account, Pinterest account, LinkedIn account and more. You can even consider creating an app (even just a simple one) which will give you visibility in the Google Play, Apple App and Windows stores. This also gives your visitors/customers another way to reach you and helps to further strengthen your brand identity (it also still impresses people).

And across all of these platforms you need to ensure that your user name is the same and that you are featuring your branding prominently. This means that your cover image should likely be your logo, while your profile image should be the same across every account and tied closely to the theme of your business (alternatively, you might make the profile image your logo and the cover image something to-do with your brand). Either way, you are working to create as consistent an experience as possible across the net so that people know what to expect when they deal with you and so that you become immediately recognizable and familiar.

"All of us need to understand the importance of branding. We are CEOs of our own companies: Me Inc. To be in business today, our most important job is to be head marketer for the brand called You."

- Tom Peters in Fast Company

Building Trust

Now you have your logo and brand and you should have a consistent design throughout your website, your social media channels and even your business card. You are reinforcing your brand at every possible opportunity and you are giving people plenty of ways to find your business and to remember you exist.

You need to ensure that the opinions being formed about your brand are positive so that people actually want to deal with you again. This goes for online businesses as well as brick and mortar businesses. Let me give you an example of a branding crisis in a brick and mortar business.

> "I can recall living Riverdale Georgia, a suburb outside of Atlanta, and walking into a business to inquire about getting some t-shirts made for an upcoming event. When I walked inside the establishment I noticed that the place looked like a scene from the early 70's. The walls were covered with brown paneling, with an abundance of non-business related photos, and the colors were very dark. I said to myself 'this can't be a design studio.' Where was the creative ideas or the artistic look we've come to expect? As I looked around the place I noticed that every product known to man was visible which

gave a confusing impression of what this company offered. The owner was tucked behind the counter in somewhat of a trance. As I walked out the door I said, "This business needs a new image."

One of the main objectives of a brand is to create a 'seal of quality'. This way, whenever someone buys something from you they should feel confident that it will be the same quality as the products they've bought from you in the past. They should feel similarly about any of your services.

Let's look at an example about 'seal of quality' and the perception of a brand. Payless, the shoe store that sells affordable shoes realized it had a branding crisis. Historically, the store has been known as America's discount footwear retailer which caused most people to think of their products as cheap and poorly made. That's not how the company wanted to be known but branding isn't just about what you put out there it's also about the perception of your customer. To change the perception of customers Payless created a marketing stunt. They created a new brand name called "Palessi." Payless used social media influencers and sold them the same shoes it sells at its store under the luxury brand for hundreds of dollars. In turn the influencers promoted this fake brand on social media. In fact, they offered testimonials about the high quality and style of the product. This marketing campaign led to the product flying off the shelves, a product that in reality cost five times less at its Payless stores. Before the marketing event was over, Payless revealed to social media influencers that the luxury brand "Palessi" shoes were in fact the same shoes sold at Payless. The influencers were given their money back and the marketing stunt went viral. With this event, Payless was able to change public perception about the quality of the shoes that it sells. With a creative marketing campaign

Payless reinvented itself as America's QUALITY discount footwear retailer. The rebranding and reposition of its brand cost Payless hundreds of thousands of dollars. What's worse is that Payless lost millions, in fact, it filed for bankruptcy because of the branding crisis.

This is why it's so important that you work hard to ensure you are delivering quality time after time. You're going to be stamping your logo onto everything you do so remember this when you put things out there. Think of everything you create as an ambassador for everything else you create. If you aren't proud of something you've created then you need to either stop selling it, or try adding to it to bring it up to standard.

Content Marketing and Becoming an Authority

This is particularly true for bloggers and internet marketers. Here, you should think of your content as your 'product'. This includes the content on your blog, any YouTube channel or podcast, and etc.

Even if you have another product that you are actually selling (digital or physical) your articles and blog posts are still products too. They are what your visitors are going to use to judge your knowledge, expertise and honesty.

This is why it's so important to make sure that you are posting in a way that strengthens your brand and that helps to build consistency and reliability. This is what content marketing is all about and it is what will allow you and your brand to establish the trust of your readers so that you can then start selling to them.

Say you were creating a fitness blog to sell an eBook, how would you do this with content marketing?

One good strategy would be to post twice a week and to make every single post unique and fascinating. Look at the competition and see what they're doing wrong and then make sure you do it better – that might mean that the subjects you tackle are more unique than the majority. Or, perhaps it just means that you're going to do more research and go more in-depth? Either way, you need to ensure that every time someone comes away from your article they are impressed and they feel that they got something they wouldn't have gotten elsewhere.

This 'style' and commitment then becomes your calling card and it is what will make people seek you out for information. It's also then what will make those same people more likely to want to buy from you when you say that you are giving away even more amazing secrets in an eBook or when you say that you highly recommend product X.

Consistency is key here and so too is a commitment to your values and to your USP (unique selling point). Make sure that each article and blog post stands alone as a testament to why you should be considered an expert and why your audience should trust you.

Note as well that you can also reinforce the association with your brand in your content. Try to mention your company/website name from time to time and to speak about yourself and this way people will be reminded about your brand as you are delivering value.

Creating Relationships

Another way you build trust is by trying to engage with your audience/customers and to build a relationship. This is one of the reason that those bloggers who have a personal brand do so well – they allow the visitors to put a face to the content they're reading and this makes them seem much more transparent and honest. As a rule, we don't put our face on things unless we believe in them.

Likewise, speaking about yourself can again help to create this trust as can showing some 'behind the scenes' of how you put your business together. The more upfront you are with your visitors and customers, the more they will think of you as an honest resource they can trust.

You can also create a relationship with your website visitors by interacting with them. This might mean asking questions in your blog posts and responding in your comments section, or it might mean surveying your audience via social media or an e-mail shout out. This is why both these marketing tools are so powerful and effective.

Under Promise and Over Deliver

You also build your relationship through your service and the way you interact with customers. One thing that can go a long way to making you seem more trustworthy and to increasing the way the general public see your brand is by taking an 'under promise and over deliver' approach.

Basically what this means is that you are offering a certain amount of value and then delivering more. One obvious way you can do this is by improving on your delivery times. Tell your customers they will get their product in 3-4 working days and then make sure it gets there in 2. They'll then be so impressed, they'll be much more inclined to want to work with you again.

Giving away free gifts is also a good way to do this. If you've ever bought a phone case on eBay you may have received a free capacitive stylus – this is the same principle in action.

Finally, Pat Flynn talks about potentially recording personal messages for people who order e-mail courses and eBooks.

This is such a nice personal touch and it goes so far in showing you went the extra mile, that it's bound to build a lot of good will and brand loyalty.

Increasing Brand Loyalty

Building trust and strengthening your brand will immediately increase your brand loyalty but there are other things you can do as well to try and turn your first time customers into repeat customers and your one-time visitors into repeat visitors.

One obvious example is to use some kind of reward or loyalty scheme. This way, when someone buys your product or service you will be able to offer them a discount or an extra incentive for buying again. Likewise, you can also achieve increased brand loyalty by upselling and giving your customers ways to increase their order. This might even go as far as creating your own 'ecosystem' or your own 'walled garden'.

This is something that Microsoft, Google, Amazon and Apple all do to varying extents. When you buy a product like an iPhone for instance, you will then likely buy apps for that device which will only run on iOS devices. This in turn means that those customers have an incentive to remain with Apple – otherwise all the money they spent on apps will be wasted. Likewise, if you buy a Windows Phone, then you might have extra reason to get a Microsoft Band – as the Microsoft Band has added functionality for Windows Phone users.

You can also give away promotional gifts as a way to enhance brand loyalty. This might mean giving your customers t-shirts with your logo on it for instance or mugs with the same branding. Either way, this has the effect of enabling you to 'over deliver' once again and at the same time means that your customers and visitors will be able to feel like a 'part of something'. Essentially, as soon as someone puts on a T-shirt with your company name on it, they will feel more as though they are true fans of your business and they will increase their brand loyalty (of course this is also free marketing!).

Finally, make sure you create a mailing list. With a mailing list you can use e-mail marketing which will allow you to reach out to your previous visitors and customers. In doing so you can remind them of your brand, bringing you to mind once again and you can encourage them to come back to your business by offering deals and discounts. E-mail marketing is highly effective because it is not reliant on social media accounts or on your fans remembering to check in with your website – you can reach them directly and right in their inboxes!

> Branding demands commitment; commitment to continual re-invention; striking chords with people to stir their emotions; and commitment to imagination. It is easy to be cynical about such things, much harder to be successful."
>
> – Sir Richard Branson

Marketing Your Brand

Building trust is all good and well but it won't help much if no one is buying your products in the first place or visiting your website.

This is where marketing your brand comes in and where you need to start thinking about how you are going to introduce people to the website, logo and products you've spent so long putting together.

Content Marketing for Exposure

We've already talked about how you can use content marketing to build trust but what's also important is using content marketing to gain exposure and traffic. Here, you are essentially using your content as an incentive to get people to visit your website and this can be a highly effective method.

The most obvious way to use content marketing is to create posts that offer value in your industry or niche and then to share links to those posts on social media, forums and social bookmarking sites.

A great place to share your content is on Facebook and Google+ which also has a 'communities' system in place. This is again a way you can potentially get hundreds or thousands of views from a single post.

Sharing Your Content on Social Media

In terms of how to get traffic to your website, social media is the next big key. You need to make sure you share your content the right way so that you get highest increase in traffic.

Here are some tips for sharing your content so that you get the most engagement, shares, and traffic:

Tip #1: Optimize for each platform

Social media posts appear differently on different platforms. So, you need to optimize your posts so that each can be eye-catching and shareable.

For example, for Facebook, a great post constitutes the following:

- A high quality photo
- Quality description (according to a study by TrackMaven, posts with 80+ words get 2X as much engagement
- A compelling link description underneath the photo
- Do your research and learn how to optimize your posts for the other social media platforms as well, so you can get a higher amount of shares, engagement, and traffic.

Tip #2: Create a sharing schedule

How often are you sharing content on social media? That's where a sharing schedule comes into play. This schedule helps keep you organized, so you're not over-sharing or under-sharing your content.

Your schedule should answer the following questions:

- Which social messages are sent immediately after publishing content? For which platforms?

- Which messages are sent the next day?
- Which messages are sent in a month? Two months?
- With a consistent schedule, you won't have to scramble every time you post new content. You'll know exactly which platforms to post on and when to post.

Tip #3: Don't spam

If a post doesn't pick up steam the first time you share it, don't try to keep reposting it the same way.

This is spam behavior and will turn your audience away if you keep doing it.

Instead, aim for a good mix of social media content – share blog posts and videos, as well as content from other influencers, and also share other interesting and value-adding statuses.

Tip #4: Add sharing buttons to your website

Sharing your content out the right way is important – but an added bonus is if you can get your audience to share it straight from your website. To do that, you need some easy social sharing buttons.

There are plenty of free social media share buttons on WordPress. Select the one you like best, and place the share buttons directly below your articles.

Tip #5: Post during peak hours

According to Hubspot, here are the best times to post to the biggest social media platforms:

(Note: Snapchat isn't listed here, but you should be posting throughout the day on that platform!)

Facebook: Weekends between 12:00 – 1:00 p.m.; Wednesdays between 3:00 – 4:00 p.m.; Thursdays and Fridays between 1:00 – 4:00 p.m.

Twitter: Mondays through Fridays between 12:00 – 3:00 p.m.; Wednesdays between 5:00 – 6:00 p.m.

LinkedIn: Tuesdays, Wednesdays, and Thursdays at: 7:30 – 8:30 a.m., 12:00 p.m., and 5:00 – 6:00 p.m. Plus, Tuesdays between 10:00 – 11:00 a.m.

Pinterest: Evening hours everyday and 2:00 – 4:00 p.m.; Fridays at 5:00 p.m.; Saturdays from 8:00 – 11:00 p.m.

Instagram: Anytime Monday through Thursday, except between 3:00 – 4:00 p.m.

Stand out with Quora

Dominating with Quora is one of the best ways to become an authority in your industry and increase your website traffic.

The format is quite simple: People ask questions, and you post answers. And if you post good answers with relevant links back to your site, you can receive a big boost in traffic.

Here's how can you start dominating with Quora:

1) Open a Quora account. Go to Quora.com and create an account.

2) Create and optimize Your Bio. Your bio is what people see when they click your profile. So, optimize it by adding a few sentences about yourself and your experience in your industry, as well as a link to your website.

3) Select relevant categories. Quora offers thousands of categories for you to choose from. Choose carefully, because your Quora feed will be filled with questions based on these categories. Aim to add at least 10-15 relevant categories.

4) Search for great questions. This is key. The better the question, the better the chance your answer will go viral

and bring you thousands and thousands of visitors. What constitutes a great question? Look for the following:

- Correct grammar
- Nice formatting (i.e. bold, italics, etc. Not just a giant block of hard-to-read text)
- Relevance to your industry
- Are fairly new (don't have any great answers yet)

5) Post strong answers. You must follow up those great questions with strong answers of your own. Here's how you can write a strong Quora answer:

- Use the first few lines to hook them in. Users can only see the first 3-4 lines in their feed, so you need to hook them from the beginning so they'll click on your answer.
- Tell stories. Some of the best Quora answers contain personal stories of beating obstacles and figuring out problems.
- Use correct grammar and formatting. If your answer isn't scannable and easy to read, users probably won't bother reading it.
- Add relevant links back to your site. Throughout your answer, sprinkle a few relevant links back to your website. The more relevant they are to the question, the more clicks and traffic they will generate. You can also end your answers with a link to your lead magnet, concluding with something like: "Want to know more about how to start a business? Check out my free checklist with 10 steps for starting your first business!" and link to the lead magnet (in this example, the checklist).
- Used right, Quora can be a powerful traffic generator for your website. And unlike most other social media, a viral Quora answer can generate steady traffic to your

website for a year or more. So, make sure not to overlook this platform.

Post and Promote on Reddit!

Reddit is another powerful, yet underused social media platform that can increase website traffic. If you can find where your audience hangs out on Reddit, and deliver the right content, you can generate tens of thousands of visits literally overnight.

So, how do you find your customers on Reddit and promote your content the right way?

Use this 2-step strategy:

Step #1: Find Your Relevant Subreddits

1) Once you go to Reddit.com, use the search box in the top right hand corner of the screen.

2) Search for a relevant keyword and hit "enter".

3) From here, you'll find a list of subreddits related to the keyword. Skim through each one and subscribe to those you think are a good match.

4) Repeat this process for the most relevant keywords related to your business.

Got it? These will be your target subreddits. These are the places your audience hangs out on Reddit.

Step #2: Post and Add Value

Once you know your target subreddits, it's time to start posting.

(Note: before you post in a subreddit, make sure to look at the posting rules for that subreddit on the right sidebar.)

You should include a few elements in your posting strategy:

1) Answers questions and respond to comments in popular threads. This will build your reputation.

2) Post a link to one article per week in the most relevant subreddit (if you can get 100-200+ upvotes on the link, you can expect upwards of 2,000-3,000 visits depending on the subreddit)

3) Always focus on adding value. Balance your links with good advice so you don't appear spammy.

4) Mix it up. Don't just submit links to Reddit. Switch it up and add text versions of your blog posts or advice, then, add a link to your post at the end.

5) Post at the right time. Let's say you want to post in the r/Entrepreneur/ subreddit, but there's already a post in the #1 spot with 200 upvotes, and it was posted 4 hours ago. If you post then, you probably won't overtake that #1 spot, and you'll get less traffic. However, if you wait a day, check back, and see that the new #1 spot only has 12-15 upvotes, then you have a golden opportunity. It will be much easier for you to hit the #1 spot and get hundreds of upvotes.

TACTICS TO SUCCEED ON SOCIAL MEDIA

1. RESIST THE PRESSURE

There is tremendous pressure for companies to develop a social media presence. Feeling the crunch, companies will just jump in.

This approach is a significant time and money-sink. Social media is just like any other marketing channel in that it requires a thoughtful, ROI focused strategy. Don't jump in.

2. PICK THE RIGHT NETWORKS FOR YOU

No Facebook? No problem. Develop a social media presence on the networks that align most strongly with your customer base and brand. Don't feel like you need to drop six figures on a Facebook presence where your customers are already likely to be hanging out.

Remember that social media is, at its heart, a distribution channel. To spread the word about your brand, you absolutely need an audience.

3. START WITH YOUR CUSTOMERS

In order for people to follow you, you need to follow your customers. Pick social networks that align most strongly with where your customers are hanging out already. If you're running a B2B organization, for instance, participation on LinkedIn Discussion Groups is a no-brainer.

If you're running a publishing website, it's mission-critical that you get your act together on Twitter, since audiences consistently tweet and re-tweet through this channel.

An e-commerce site, on the other hand, may see stronger results on Facebook (that is, unless your customer base is active on Twitter). It really depends on your customers' preferences, internet browsing, patterns, and demographic. For photographers and travel bloggers, for instance, it makes sense to use Instagram since the social media platform specializes in photos.

When in doubt, run an informal research study or just ask.

4. INVEST IN BUILDING A COMMUNITY

Online communities add value in the form of exposure and distribution. A portion of your fans and followers are likely to convert. When you invest in building up your social media following, you are investing in distribution.

Focus on building your fan base by asking your audience to become a fan or follower in order to read the rest of your content:

Just like email marketing, it's important to build your following organically. When audiences opt into becoming a fan, they're more likely to engage with your brand on an ongoing basis.

Be respectful when recruiting fans and followers. Some folks just won't want to. Make sure that there's an opportunity to opt-out. Include a "No Thanks" link. You will want to cookie your readers to make sure that after they see the invitation once, they don't again.

This strategy can help you double your social media following — which can easily evolve into 30% to 40% of your overall website traffic.

5. BUILD YOUR EMAIL LIST ON SOCIAL MEDIA

Use a tool like 5 Minute Fan Page to collect leads on your Facebook page. These lead generation forms have the potential to achieve much higher conversion rates than they do off Facebook.

Another approach is to collect email addresses through Facebook Connect:

Expect to pay $0.25 to $1 per email address collected. If your email marketing strategy is well integrated with your conversion goals, you should be able to make your money back relatively quickly. Not to mention, an email list is something with long-term value. Every time you have a new product or announcement, you can instantly promote that message to your list.

6. TIME YOUR MESSAGING PERFECTLY

Obviously, a 2AM Facebook post is unlikely to recruit eyeballs. Beyond the obvious, however, it's important to pay attention to the nuances of timing your posts. Use free social media tools from Simply Measured to time your Tweets and status updates just right. Post when audiences are most likely to be engaging with your social sites.

7. SYNC UP WITH GREAT CONTENT

Social media and content marketing go hand in hand. When people are browsing their Facebook and Twitter feeds, they're not necessarily in the mood to buy. They want to be social, catch up with friends, connect with family, browse pictures, and relax.

As much as you want to sell, your content shouldn't. They key is to build audience relationships instead. People make laugh. Capture their interest. Be a brand that is also a friend. Share content, not products. Remember that people are emotional and want to be entertained.

And yes, that sometimes means sharing a meme or two.

Promote content beyond your own. Curate content from the community, and share what's most relevant to your friends and followers. Clarity does a great job exemplifying this concept by curating amazing reads from entrepreneurs and business leaders.

8. DRIVE ENGAGEMENT

Once audiences browse through your content, make sure to connect them with more. This strategy is especially important for YouTube videos.

Get more video views by ending your video with another. You'll need a video editor to create these modifications.

9. HOST ONLINE EVENTS

This strategy can help build loyalty and engagement. Host tweet-ups to help answer your fans' most pressing questions. Other ideas include follower-only webinars and Facebook networking parties to help businesses connect with one another.

10. JUMP INTO CONVERSATIONS

Be social. Join Quora and LinkedIn discussion groups to build trust and awareness about your brand. If somebody asks questions related to your product, provide an answer. If your company can solve a specific problem, make sure that the community knows.

11. ASK QUESTIONS

Conversations go both ways. Ask questions as much as you're broadcasting messages. Questions can help you better understand your customers and show how much you care. Conduct market intelligence, learn what people think of your products, and get people talking.

This approach can also help you brainstorm topics for your content marketing, blogging, or infographic strategy.

12. CAPTURE ATTENTION WITH IMAGES

People don't want to read chunks of text. They want easy-to-scan, attention-grabbing images. Get creative, and don't afraid to be funny — even if you're a little off base from your brand. Just don't be boring.

13. ANALYSE THE SUCCESS OF YOUR CONTENT

Like any marketing channel, social media ROI should be measured and tracked. Make sure to segment your data by post-type (content vs. deals vs. products), and keep track of your long-term user value. With social media, conversions are much less likely to be direct.

Virality is another metric that you should watch. When people share your content with their fans and followers, your company gets free marketing.

KEY TAKEAWAYS

- Choose social channels that align with your audience.

- Don't feel obligated to launch social media profiles that are misaligned with your brand.

- Track results so that you can make optimizations and continuously improve performance.

- Monitor metrics related to virality, engagement, leads and conversions, and costs.

- Shares and re-tweets are extremely valuable because they generate free exposure for your company.

- Encourage users to share your content by implementing (and testing the placement of) social sharing widgets.

- Be as visual as you possibly can. People don't like to read giant blocks of text.

- Remember that people on social media aren't necessarily in the mindset to shop. They're looking to connect with friends, sync up with family, browse photos, and discover entertaining media.

- Integrate your social media strategy with your branded content program. Content is a powerful referral traffic driver.

Guest Posting

Another way to use content marketing to get your brand seen by new people is with guest posting. Guest posts are posts that appear on blogs but which are written by someone other than the owner of that blog.

So in other words, you are going to find a blog in your niche that is doing particularly well and then ask them to publish a post or article you've written. You're giving the content away for free (which benefits them by filling their blog with more value) but in exchange you're asking that there be a link embedded in the post back to your site.

This can do wonders for helping you to build brand recognition and gain traffic to your website. For starters, having a link on a prominent blog is very good for SEO (search engine optimization) as long as you don't 'overdo' this strategy. At the same time though, your link and your company/business name is now going to be seen by hundreds or thousands of people who visit that blog and is effectively going to be given testimony by the author of that blog. If they trust the blogger, then some of this trust will be passed on to you and you will benefit from association. See how this works?

Advertising

Another way to get your brand out there is through plain and simple advertising. There are plenty of options here when you're online but one of the best is to use PPC marketing. PPC stands for 'Pay Per Click' and is essentially a form of advertising where you only get charged if someone actually clicks on your ads. This means that ineffectual ads are not charged and that means you can get your ad seen completely for free – thus building brand awareness at no cost to you.

The biggest two platforms for PPC are Google's AdWords platform and Facebook ads. These allow you to advertise right on the SERPs (search engine results pages) or on Facebook respectively and also let you target your audience either by advertising on particular search terms or by filtering through age, hobbies, gender etc.

In either case, you should try to sell a particular product through your advert and you should be as upfront and honest as this as possible. A good advert on Facebook or AdWords will simply say 'Click here to buy $30 fitness eBook!'.

This way, a large proportion of the people who click on that ad will be willing to part with their money meaning you'll get a good ROI (especially as you only pay a few cents for each ad). But for those who don't click, you're still going to be showing your logo which means you'll still be increasing awareness and visibility.

Out of the two, Facebook advertising potentially makes more sense here because it lets you use your images which means you can incorporate your actual logo. Another alternative is to try Google AdSense which is a similar product that allows your adverts to appear on the websites of participating publishers. You choose which website to appear on by niche and can then choose from either text or banner ads.

SEO

SEO is 'Search Engine Optimization' or in other words, the process of getting a website to rank highly on Google when someone searches for a related term. SEO goes hand in hand with content marketing because you can use keywords in your content in order to help target certain search terms. In other words, by including just a few mentions of the phrase 'buy hats' in your article on fashion, you can help people who are interesting in 'buying hats' to find your website via another article.

Likewise, you can target specific questions – a web designer for instance might write an article on how to set up a

WordPress website, use SEO to help people looking for that term to find that post, and then hope that people reading the content will be impressed enough to consider hiring them to handle it on their behalf. (Don't overdo the insertion of keywords – optimal keyword 'density' is generally thought to be about 1-2%)

SEO should also be used though simply to ensure that your business and website appears at the top of Google when someone searches for it. Using SEO is a way to ensure that when someone types in 'Keywords related to your business', your site will come up. This way, someone who is somewhat interested in your business will be able to easily research you to find out more and possibly to get in touch and hire you for your services.

How can you achieve this:

a) by using your company name throughout your site (and as your URL)

b) by making sure you submit yourself to business directories and set up a Google+ My Business page.

All this will also help to give you further credibility as a serious brand.

Press Releases

When you launch your new business or website, you should issue a press release to inform any websites or other outlets that might be interested in covering the story. This is a great way to get free publicity and to get some good momentum when you first announce your new business or website. *Note however that press releases will only work if your story is genuinely newsworthy*. If it's not, then try to paint it in a light that makes it interesting and something people would want to read about.

Email Marketing to build up Connections

Email marketing is one of the most effective and inexpensive ways to find and keep new customers. Email Marketing is the process of sending e-mails to acquire new customers and convince existing customers to make additional purchases. It is also used to enhance the relationship of a business with its customers and prospects and encourage customer loyalty and repeat business.

Think about it. When you send an email, you reach your audience in one of the most personalized ways possible. Our email inboxes are literally in the palms of our hands. We're glued to email at work, after work, first thing in the morning, and right before bed. It's an understatement to say that email is a powerful marketing channel.

By building a mailing list, a business can create an extremely valuable asset.

The advantages of email:

- Email lets you send information to a wide range of existing and potential customers at a much lower cost than direct mail or printed newsletters.

- E-mail marketing allows you to track your return on investment exactly and is often reported as second only to search marketing as the most effective online marketing tactic.

- The delivery time for an e-mail message is short (i.e., seconds or minutes) as compared to a mailed advertisement (i.e., one or more days).

- E-mail marketing is paper-free (i.e., "green)

- Once you have a large list, you can "rent" your list to 3rd party marketing firms that will mail other offers to people on your list - this can be a significant additional source of revenue for your business.

Even with all the junk out there, email marketing still has ROI. According to an Consultancy study, two-thirds of marketers rate the ROI from email marketing as 'excellent' or 'good.'

Build Personal Connections

- Questions in subject lines are a great way to build a rapport/inspire a connection
- Be matter-of-fact and upfront
- Inspire dialogue from the get-go
- Don't give up. When you cold pitch prospects, rejections are bound to happen. Continually follow up until you get a response. It took me 6 months to get Michael Arrington to hire me.
- Be thorough. The more that you can show real examples and solutions to your prospects' problems, the more credible you'll appear as a resource.
- Don't be afraid to name drop previous clients and connections that you have in common.
- Be respectful. Sometimes people will ignore you, and that's okay. Even if you persist, they'll still ignore you, and that's ok. Just move on, and don't feel bad about it. It's their loss, not yours.

Personal connections will help you fight the spam effect. Focus your message directly to your end recipient. Make them care.

BALANCE PERSONALIZATION WITH AUTOMATION

Imagine sending tens of thousands of individualized emails to your marketing list.

You probably can't because it's impossible.

That's the beauty of marketing automation software. Send emails to the right users (and customer/prospect segments) at just the right time in the purchase cycle. It's a sophisticated way to scale personal attention.

The key to successful marketing automation is technology. Rely on tools (rather than spreadsheet) to reach your email list successfully. The biggest players in the space include:

- Convertkit
- aWeber
- MailChimp
- Mailerlite
- InfusionSoft

1. UNDERSTAND CUSTOMER NEEDS

Customers have more tools than ever to filter out unwanted messaging with priority inboxes. Your deliverability statistics may be strong, but your emails are getting ignored for reasons outside of your control. You need to build a connection with your audience before you start sending them emails. Implement an opt-in process — a series of steps that subscribers can take to ensure that they're receiving your emails. Perhaps include a freebie, piece of content, or promotion/deal that they'll receive in exchange. Don't just bombard your customers with emails. Make sure that they're set up (and willing) to read what you have to say.

2. SYNC UP WITH OTHER MARKETING CHANNELS

Email should not be a standalone marketing channel. Make sure you're integrating all of your marketing campaigns. If you launch a blog, for instance, make sure to concurrently build your email list. Every time you publish a new blog post, notify your subscribers via email. This chain of events will keep audiences coming back to your website.

3. COMPLETE THE CUSTOMER EXPERIENCE

An understanding of user psychology is successful for successful email marketing (and automation especially). You need to make sure that you're targeting customers and prospects with messaging that complements their needs and intent.

Always create a plan or outline for your email marketing campaigns — make sure that your messages follow a system or schedule.

The first step is to sequence all of your emails. What messages should you be sending, and what steps should users take after each message?

4. PRIORITIZE CONVERSION OPTIMIZATION

You need to specify a clear conversion goal from your email marketing automation. You also need to ensure that your landing pages are fully optimized for the actions you want users to take.

5. OPTIMIZE EMAIL DELIVERABILITY RATES

Deliverability is important to email marketing. Make sure you're taking all possible steps to reach your audience's inbox. Here are some clear steps to take:

- Don't use the color red. It's a loud color and is used by a lot of spammers. It could set off a number of spam filters.

- Don't use misleading subject lines. Make sure they're fleshed out (don't leave them blank), and ensure that the subject matches the email body.

- Avoid capital letters Within your email and in the subject lines.

- Be smart about symbols. If you use too many, your emails will look totally spammy.

- Don't link too much. Limit your links to 3, max.

- Include unsubscribe links. This is required, by law.

- Be thorough yet to the point. Make sure you include a straightforward reply to and from email address so that subscribers can get in touch with you.

- Choose the right service provider. Some have better deliverability rates by industry.

The FTC rigorously enforces laws email compliance. Make sure that your strategy is aligned with the CAN-SPAM Act so that you're not exposed to potential lawsuits. Here are the rules that businesses must follow:

1. Don't use false or misleading header information. You're "From," "To," "Reply-To," and routing information - including the originating domain name and email address - must be accurate and identify the person or business who initiated the message.
2. Don't use deceptive subject lines. The subject line must accurately reflect the content of the message.
3. Identify the message as an ad. The law gives you a lot of leeway in how to do this, but you must disclose clearly and conspicuously that your message is an advertisement.
4. Tell recipients where you're located. Your message must include your valid physical postal address. This can be your current street address, a post office box you've registered with the U.S. Postal Service, or a private mailbox you've registered with a commercial mail receiving agency established under Postal Service regulations.
5. Tell recipients how to opt out of receiving future email

from you. Your message must include a clear and conspicuous explanation of how the recipient can opt out of getting email from you in the future. Craft the notice in a way that's easy for an ordinary person to recognize, read, and understand. Creative use of type size, color, and location can improve clarity. Give a return email address or another easy Internet-based way to allow people to communicate their choice to you. You may create a menu to allow a recipient to opt out of certain types of messages, but you must include the option to stop all commercial messages from you. Make sure your spam filter doesn't block these opt-out requests.

6. Honor opt-out requests promptly. Any opt-out mechanism you offer must be able to process opt-out requests for at least 30 days after you send your message. You must honor a recipient's opt-out request within 10 business days. You can't charge a fee, require the recipient to give you any personally identifying information beyond an email address, or make the recipient take any step other than sending a reply email or visiting a single page on an Internet website as a condition for honoring an opt-out request. Once people have told you they don't want to receive more messages from you, you can't sell or transfer their email addresses, even in the form of a mailing list. The only exception is that you may transfer the addresses to a company you've hired to help you comply with the CAN-SPAM Act.

7. Monitor what others are doing on your behalf. The law makes clear that even if you hire another company to handle your email marketing, you can't contract away your legal responsibility to comply with the law. Both the company whose product is promoted in the message and the company that actually sends the message may be held legally responsible.

MEASURE THE RIGHT METRICS

There are two types of email marketing metrics: (1) engagement and (2) conversions/monetary analysis. A healthy marketing strategy should focus on both:

ENGAGEMENT

- Total Opens: This is the total number of times an email in a campaign is opened. This is usually a count of the total number of times an invisible pixel is opened.
- Total Open Rate: This is calculated by taking the total number of email opens and dividing them by the number of delivered emails.
- Unique Opens: This is similar total opens but is limited to unique viewers (i.e. only one open per person is counted).
- Total Clicks: This measures clicks generated from each campaign. You should include your unsubscribe rate from this metric.
- Total Click-Through Rate (CTR): Divide the total number of clicks by the number of delivered emails.
- Unique Clicks: This will tell you how many unique people clicked on at least one link in the email.
- Click-to-Open Rate: This can be done specifically for mobile opens to understand the efficacy of your campaign on smartphones and tablets.
- Conversions, Conversion Rates, and Revenue: These are metrics that you should be tracking across your marketing channels.

KEY TAKEAWAYS

- Personalization is the foundation of your email marketing strategy.
- Rely on software through marketing automation to scale your 1:1 relationships.

- Do your due diligences to ensure you choose the right marketing automation software for your company and industry?
- Focus on the entire user experience, and guide email subscribers towards conversion-focused goals.
- Know federal spam laws so that your email marketing campaigns are fully compliant.
- Synchronize your email campaigns with your content marketing efforts. Build your email list from the ground up, and build a steady traffic stream to your website.
- Remember that your audience is reading emails from a variety of devices. They're not necessarily behind a computer screen.

> "The most important thing to remember is you must know your audience."
>
> – Lewis Howes

How To Manage Your Brand And Reputation

Of course with a highly recognizable brand also comes some new risks. Specifically – if everything you do is building your reputation, then every time you drop the ball this can also harm your reputation. This is how you can end up tainting your brand and having a bad reputation for your brand is pretty much toxic to your profits.

Think about Hyundai for instance. At one point, this car manufacturing company had such a bad reputation that their cars became the butt of jokes. They were thought of as unappealing, unreliable and uncool. Thus, even someone who would otherwise have been happy with specific cars they were selling, would be unlikely to want to do business with them simply because of the stigma they carried.

So what do you do if your brand has been hurt by bad reviews, by the competition or by your own mistakes?

Reputation Management

One option is reputation management, much of which is achieved through SEO. This means effectively using search engine optimization to improve the information that becomes available when someone searches for your business.

If your last few products or your recent services haven't been up to your usual standard, then this might result in some bad reviews appearing prominently in the search engine results. This in turn means that the first things people find about you will potentially be negative when they look for your brand online.

Getting your own website to be the first result when searching for your business then is obviously one way you can begin to combat this. At the same time, you can work to increase the visibility of the positive reviews that are out there to help them rise above the negative ones.

Reputation management also means other things. For example, you need to ensure that you are generating those positive reviews which you can do simply by asking your customers and visitors to. Another option is to offer incentives for good reviews – such as discounts. A good strategy on social media is to say that you will write X post or provide X product but only if you receive a certain number of likes or reviews.

It's also important to make sure you're seen to respond to negative reviews in a polite and effective manner. Express your concern that your customer was not happy with the product or service they received (even if you don't really feel that way!) and then offer to make amends in some way or other. This is reassuring for other potential customers, it demonstrates that you care and if you can solve the problem for the customer then they may even alter their review and make it more positive.

What To Do If You're Planning On Rebranding

If things have really gone south, then sometimes the only remaining option will be to completely rebrand yourself and to start the process again from scratch. This will mean creating a new logo, changing the design of your website and potentially even beginning an entirely new marketing campaign.

A rebrand can also be useful as a way to gain publicity. If your brand is relatively recognizable, then changing your name will be interesting to the general public and if you issue a press release you might get coverage this way.

Note though that rebrands will often confuse customers and can sometimes go wrong. Make sure that you do your research before setting out and are sensitive in the way you rebrand yourself. Note as well that you will also lose a lot of your previous hard work when you remarket yourself under a different name or logo – a lot of your prospective audience won't yet associate your new logo with your business and thus you'll need to work to build that recognition again.

There's also a slight stigma surrounding any rebranding as the question will always be: why did they feel the need to change their image so drastically? Make sure that you communicate clearly why you are rebranding and paint it in a positive light. I.e. you're moving with the times, not you're trying to shake those rumors that you beat your employees.

Conclusion and Recap

Online brands over the last decade and a half have disrupted industries across the world and have changed the way we do business forever.

In addition, online brands have changed people's lives. For the first time, there is a real gateway for someone who wants to exit out of their cubicle for a life where they don't feel chained to something and can actually be free.

It can happen fast, or it can happen slow.

Online marketing isn't something new for small businesses to consider anymore. In fact, it's quite the opposite... having been going on for years and seemingly has no end in sight. Yet, far too many small business owners neglect how important online marketing is for their business success. Among the reasons this seems to be is time. Another money. And yet another is that they don't care. The reality is, however, customers do care and in order to be relevant in today's crowded marketplace, being online is a must.

Having a website that's search optimized, being on social media that you actually engage with and incorporating email into your marketing strategy may seem like a hefty load to carry, but the reality is it is almost too easy for small businesses to do nowadays.

So that's it, the essentials of creating, building and managing your brand! You should now understand the importance of having a strong brand, know how to choose a company name and create a logo and have a plan in place for promoting your business/website and building trust.

There's a lot to take on board there, so just to recap let's go over some of the key points. Follow these in order and you should be well on your way to strengthening your brand and creating authority in your niche or industry.

Identify Your Goals and Mission Statement

You should have an idea of the business model you're going to be using and of the niche you're going to be in. Next, you need to identify what makes you different and what your overarching goals are. This will then serve as your mission statement which will provide your value proposition and USP and help you to create your brand.

Choose a Name

The next step is to choose a company name and buy a domain name. Make sure the name is descriptive, original and memorable and think about how this will affect your SEO down the line.

Create a Logo

Next you should create your logo. This will need to be created as a vector image to allow for editing. Create a moodboard to get ideas and try combining elements that speak to your products, niche and company name. Consider protecting your brand with a patent.

Create Your Other Materials

Your goal now is to reinforce your branding at every possible opportunity. This means creating business cards, a web design and much more all utilizing the same logo and the same colors to reinforce your brand further. Consider using your own name, face and personality as part of your marketing plan.

Be Consistent

Make sure you post to your blog regularly with high quality content. This is how you can use content marketing to establish yourself as a trust worthy resource.

At the same time, if you sell or recommend products or services, make sure that they are always high quality as well. This is what will create the association between your brand and the idea of quality and reliability – which is your main aim.

Create Brand Loyalty

Engage with your readers/customers, create a loyalty scheme and collect e-mails. This way you can turn your one-time customers into repeat buyers and those repeat buyers into hardened fans.

Market Yourself

With content marketing, SEO, social media, press releases and advertising – make sure that people see your brand regularly so that they are more likely to remember it and more likely to look for you in future.

Manage Your Brand

Make sure that you keep an eye on reviews, respond to any negative comments and consider rebranding if necessary. If you release new products, think about how you will brand those too and how they'll tie into your overall branding strategy.

And there you have it! So just keep providing value under an easily identifiable image and company and you'll find that you build a reputation for yourself that drives more traffic to your site and more business to your company.

Final Words

Lastly, despite the fact that brand building is important, especially if you want to succeed online, one must never be so consumed in perfecting a brand to the extent of losing yourself and personality all throughout the process. After all, you're going to work with people you like and trust-- not machines without emotions nor personality. It's true that brand building doesn't happen over night and it will take a lot of time and dedication in order to succeed and stand out from the crowd. By committing your time and energy as you build your brand wisely, you'll soon realize that all of the hard work and sacrifice you have made are worth it.

By the end of the day, a successful brand can make your family, current clients, and even future customers to prefer your brand-- "that thing" that only you can offer.

Are you ready to BUILD YOUR BRAND?

Don't forget the importance of branding is "Clarity"

Download this FREE #SpecialReport:

To understand what is a brand, why it's really important, and how to build a strong personal brand.

The 5-Minute Guide to Building a Incredible Brand.

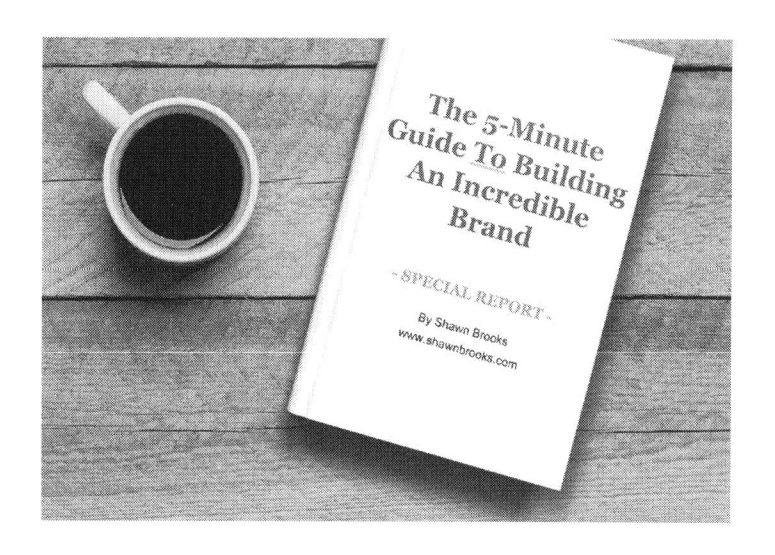

http://shawnbrooks.com/brand-builder/

Made in the USA
Columbia, SC
14 March 2021